CONSERVATION IN ACTION

The papyrus of Nakhtefmut

New life for a Book of the Dead

by Christina Rozeik

Contents

Context: the Nakhtefmut papyrus

This papyrus was found on the mummy of Nakhtefmut. He died around 890 BC and was a priest at Thebes, in ancient Egypt.

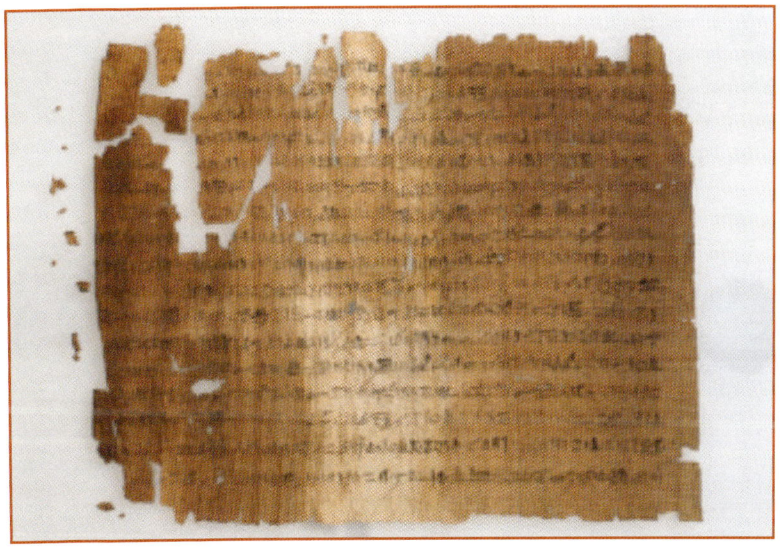

Nakhtefmut's tomb was excavated by J. E. Quibell in 1896. He describes unwrapping the mummy and finding the papyrus:

"On the thighs lay a flat sheet of papyrus written on both sides, which is, according to Dr. Spiegelberg, 'a most valuable specimen of a text of the Book of the Dead of the XXIInd dynasty'."

Quibell 1898: 11

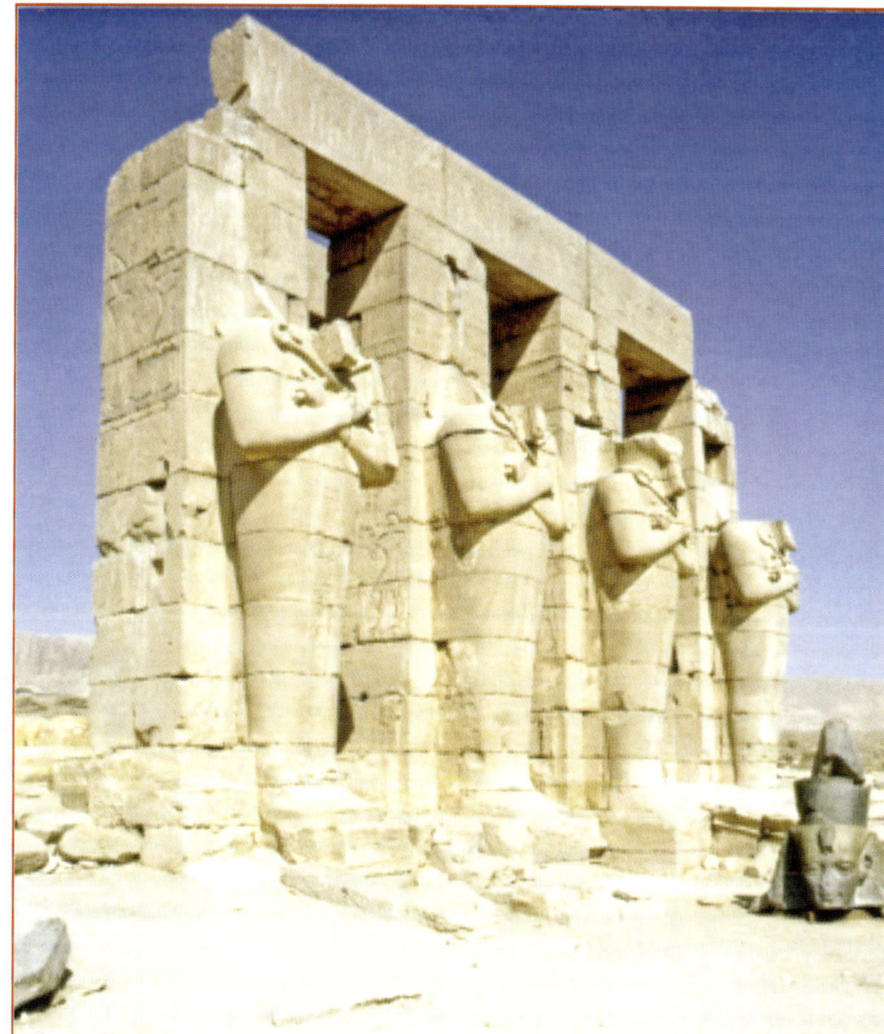

Nakhtefmut was buried in the Ramesseum in Thebes (above). His cartonnage mummy case and funerary equipment are now in the Fitzwilliam Museum in Cambridge.

Context: the Nakhtefmut papyrus

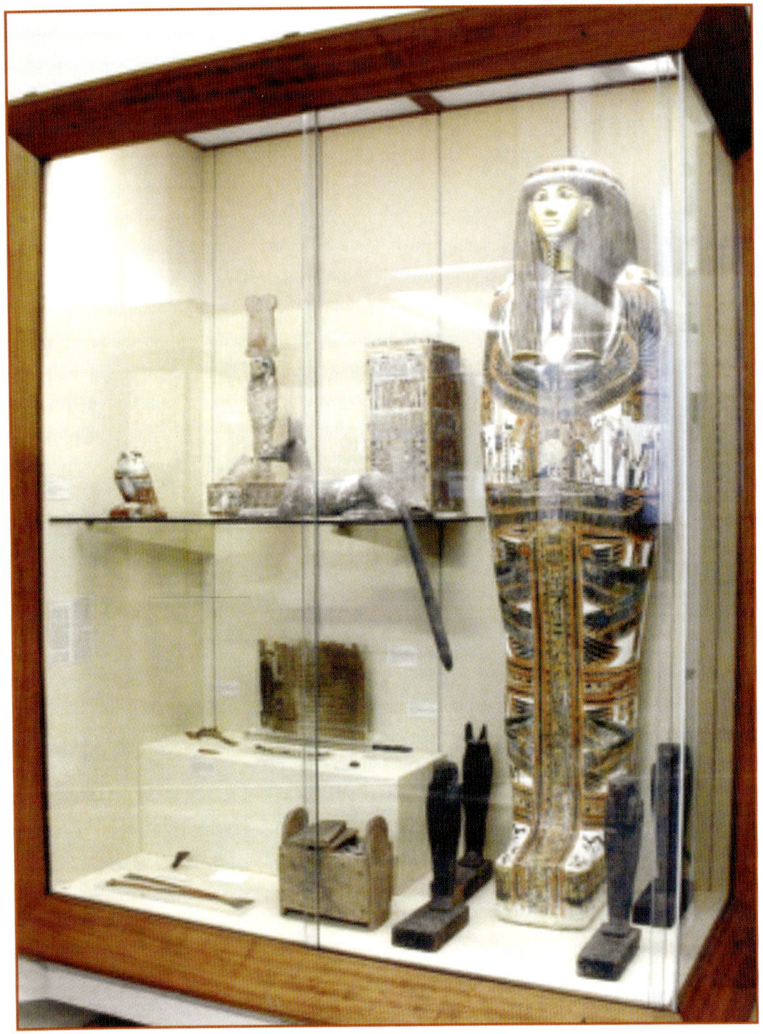

The papyrus on display in the old Egyptian galleries in the Fitzwilliam (above); the same tomb group on display in the recently refurbished galleries (right).

The papyrus was conserved for display in the Fitzwilliam Museum's new Egyptian galleries, with the other objects from Nakhtefmut's tomb.

The tomb group has been conserved, mounted and displayed as a single group. The papyrus was treated because it was dirty and badly mounted.

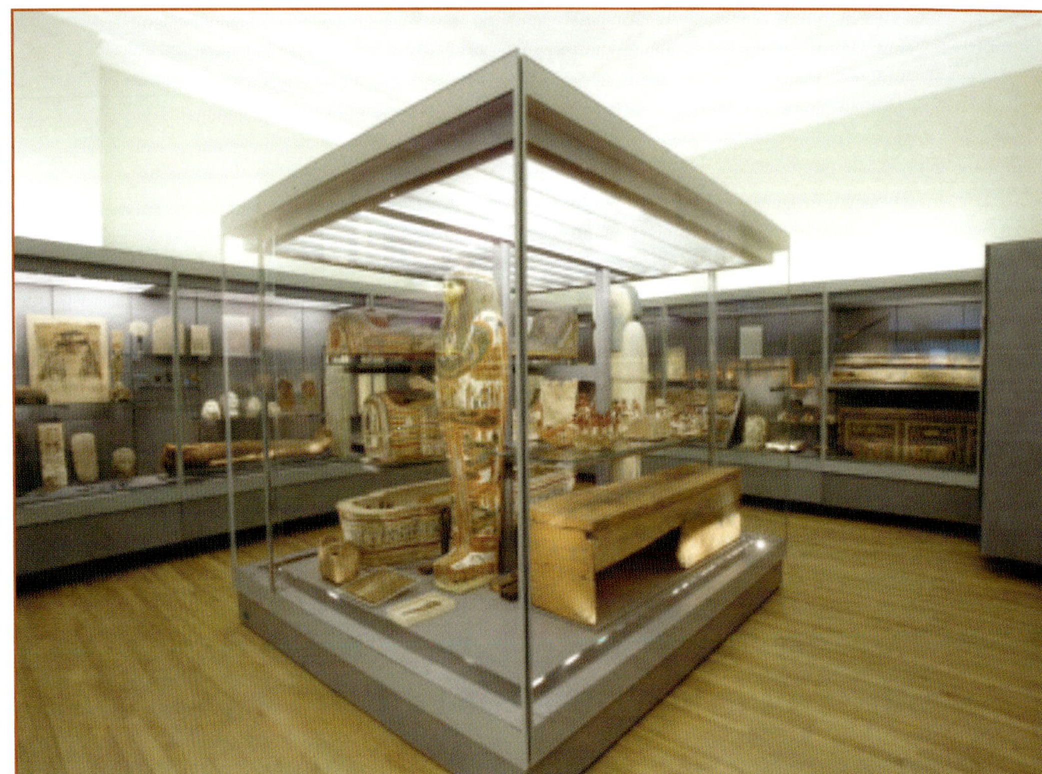

Context: the ancient Egyptian *Book of the Dead*

The ancient Egyptian *Book of the Dead* was a collection of spells, prayers and useful information, designed to help the dead pass safely through the underworld and attain everlasting life.

Spells were usually written on papyrus and buried with the dead person.

One of the spells on the Nakhtefmut papyrus says:

'Go back, you messenger of any god! … I will not let you take away this heart of mine which belongs to the living who move about …'

Chapter (spell) 29

Andrews 1995: 54

'Funerary papyri of the Third Intermediate Period (after about 1085 BC) were often written in hieratic rather than in linear hieroglyphs and in that case the text was written in horizontal lines arranged in pages not in columns.'

Andrews 1985: 15

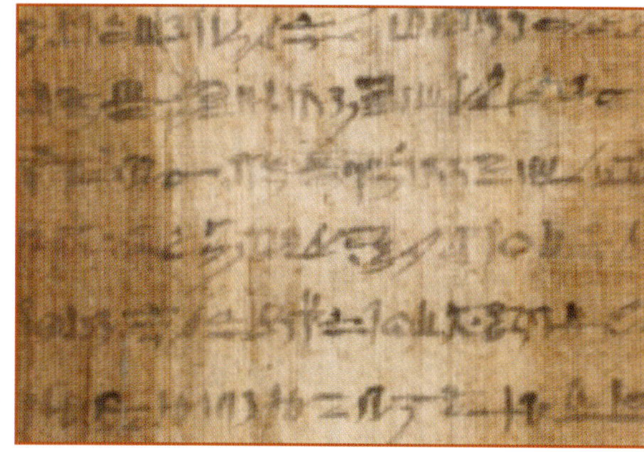

Detail showing hieratic script on the Nakhtefmut papyrus

'I think the papyrus of Nakhtefmut was the 70th chapter of the Book of the Dead. Spiegelberg copied it & I will ask him. The text of the Books of the Dead is very bad. There is no text in reception yet: and there is very little interest in the carelessly written and late copies …'

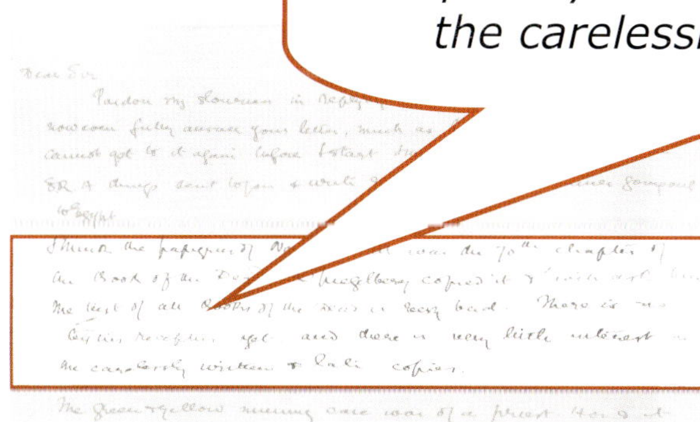

Some of the correspondence between Quibell and the Fitzwilliam Museum is still in the museum's archives.

Technology: the *Cyperus papyrus* plant

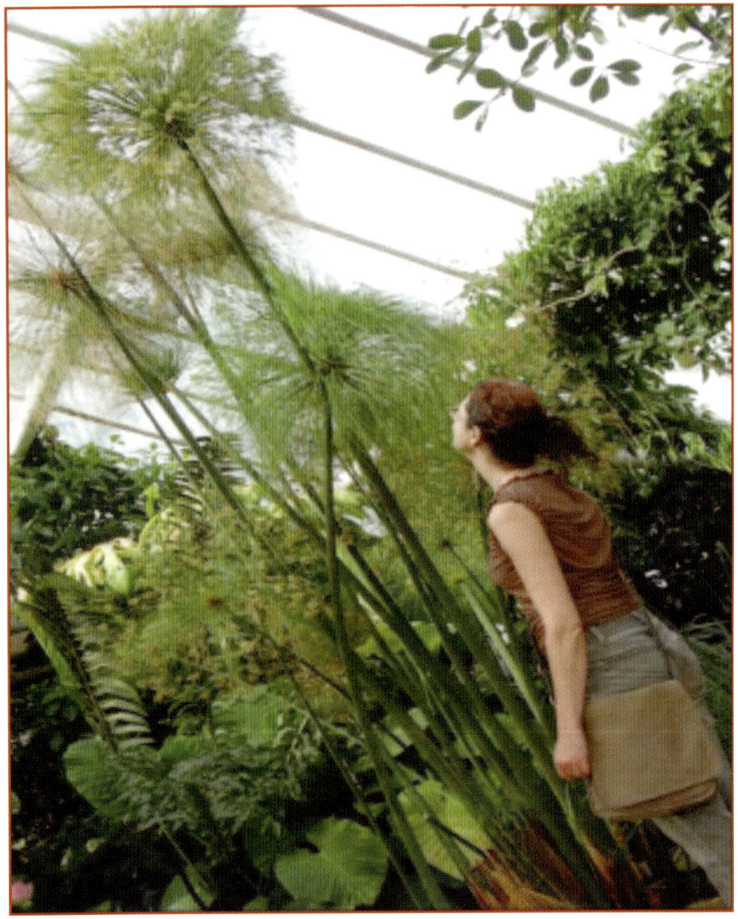

Papyrus can grow to a great height, up to 5 metres tall! The example above is from the Botanic Gardens in Cambridge.

Papyrus manufacture ceased in Egypt after the Roman period, but has recently been revived for the tourist trade using plants imported from the Sudan. The methods used have changed little between ancient and modern times.

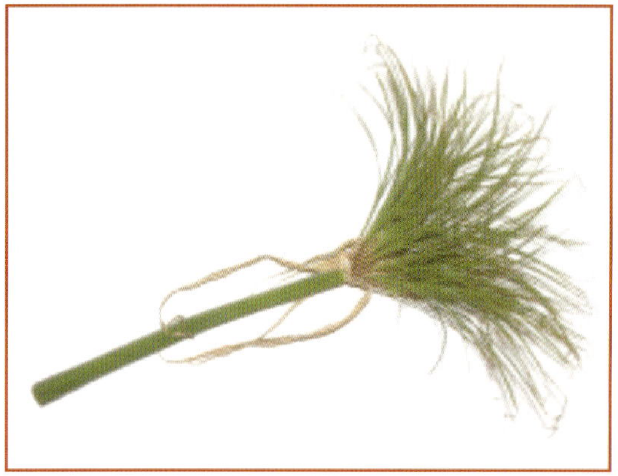

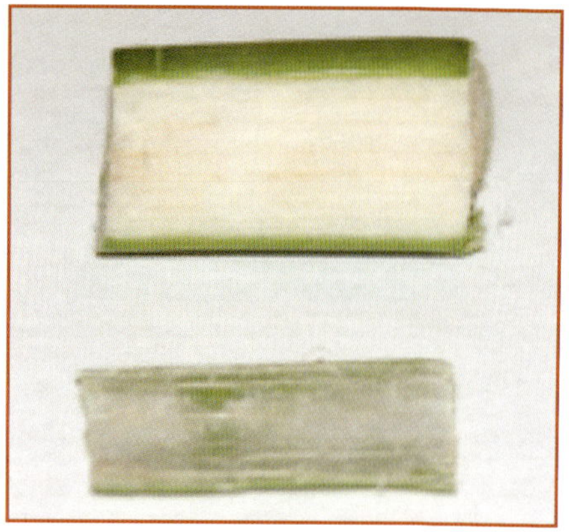

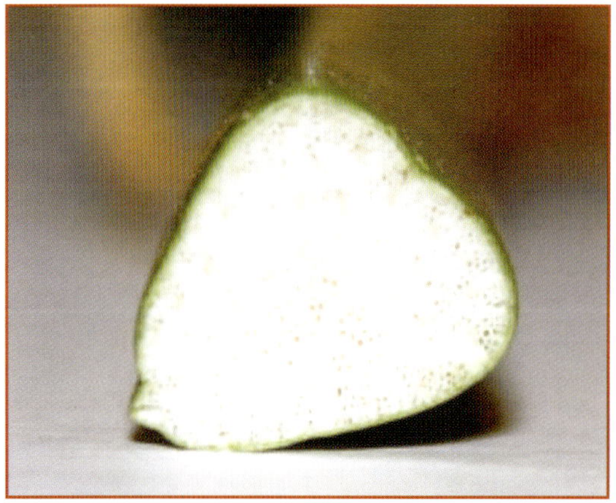

Papyrus stems have feathery tops (above left) and a distinctive triangular cross-section (left). The tough, outer rind can be cut off to reveal the soft pith inside (top right). This pith is used to make papyrus sheets.

Technology: making papyrus

The papyrus stem (*1*) is stripped of its tough outer rind (*2*); this rind may be used for making sandals or ropes. The soft inner pith is sliced thinly into long strips (*3*).

1

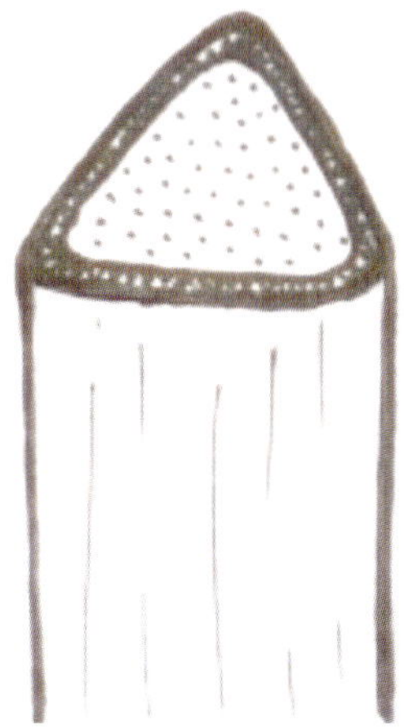

2

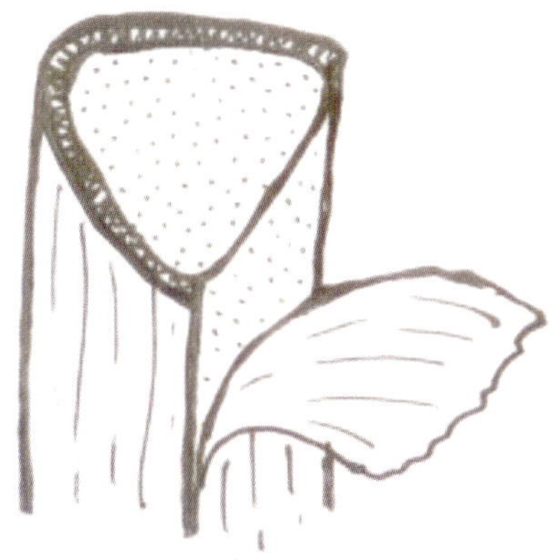

3

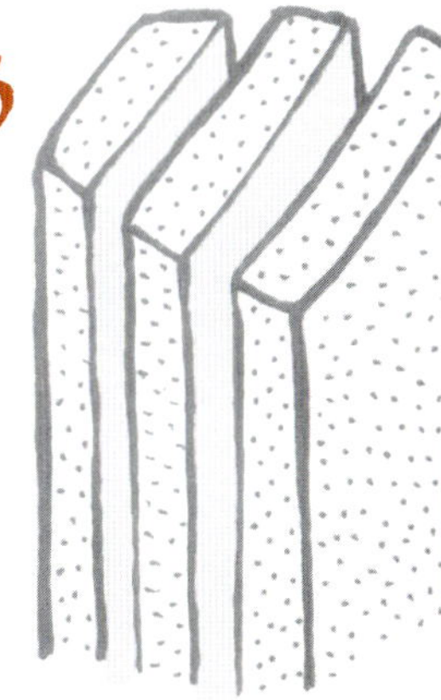

4

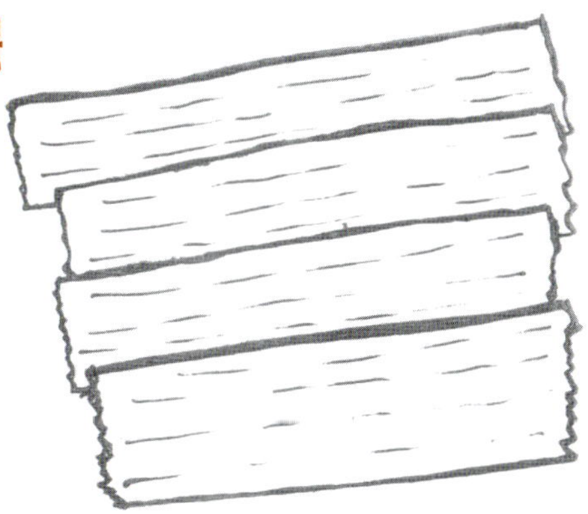

5

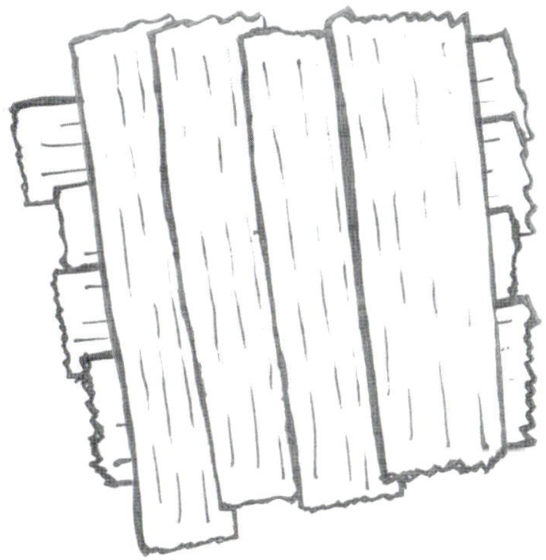

After the strips have been soaked to release their natural gums, they are laid in parallel lines, overlapping slightly (*4*). A second layer of strips is placed on top, perpendicular to the first layer (*5*). The papyrus is pressed to bond the layers together, then dried.

Conservation: condition of the papyrus before treatment

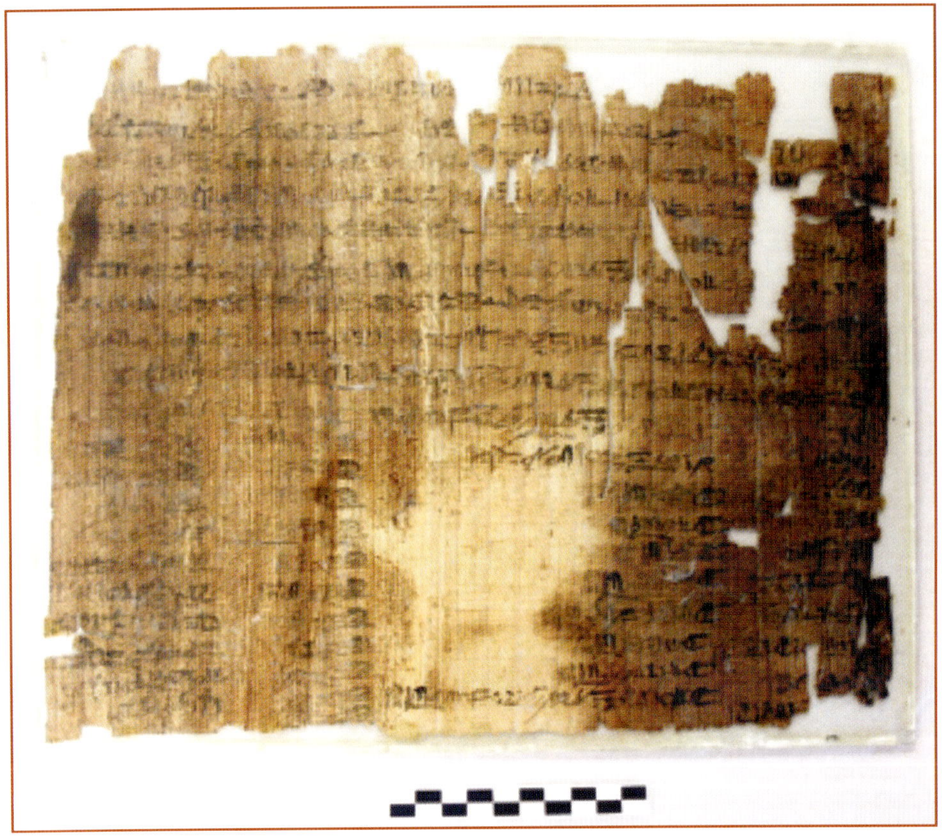

The papyrus had been on display in the Fitzwilliam Museum's old Egyptian galleries, mounted between two sheets of glass. The sheets of glass were only held together with adhesive tape, which had now lost most of its sticking power!

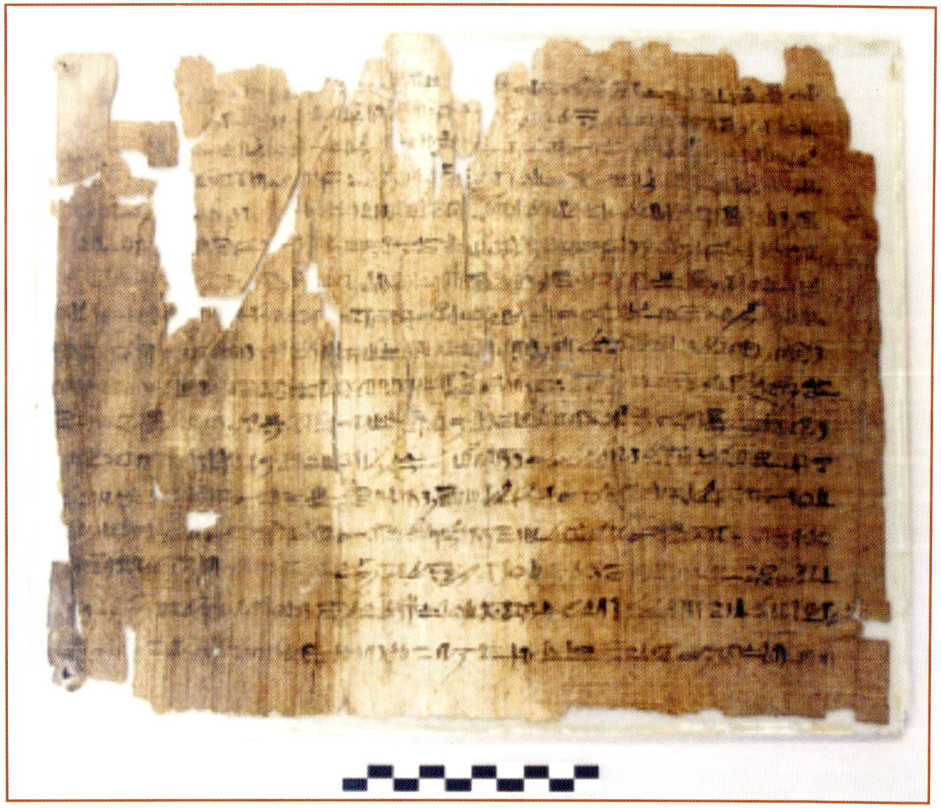

The papyrus had been stuck to one side of the glass and the adhesive used had become opaque with age. This was very unsightly and obscured some of the text. These pictures show what the two sides of the papyrus looked like before treatment.

Conservation: condition of the papyrus before treatment

The first stage of treatment was to make detailed drawings of the papyrus showing what it looked like before conservation.

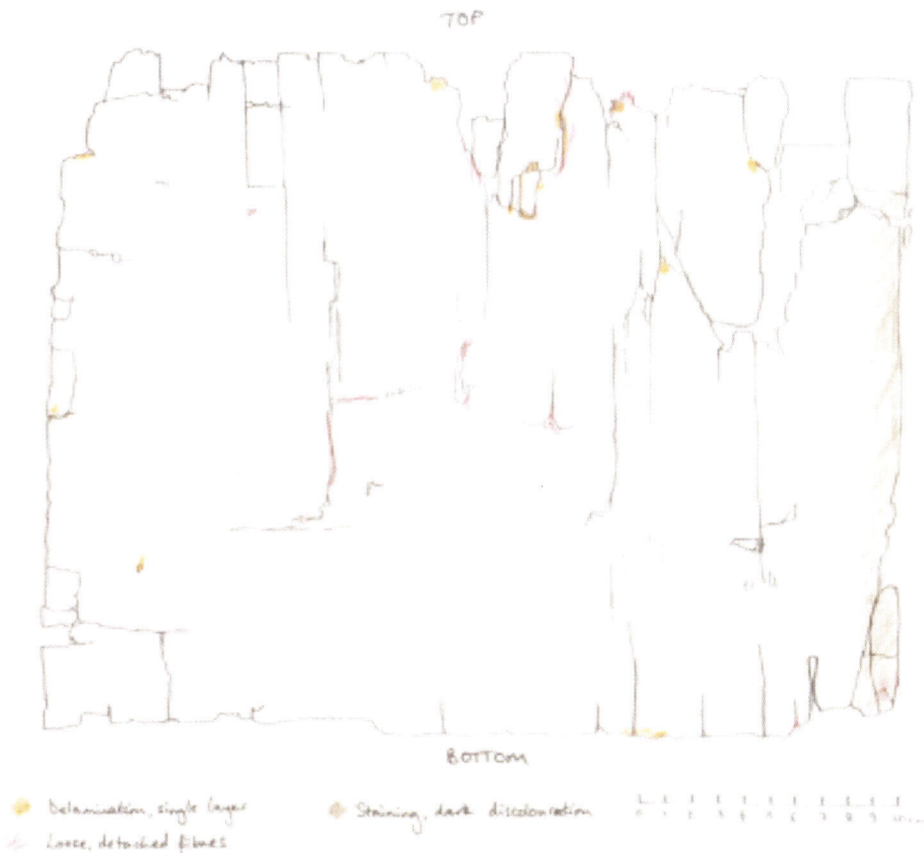

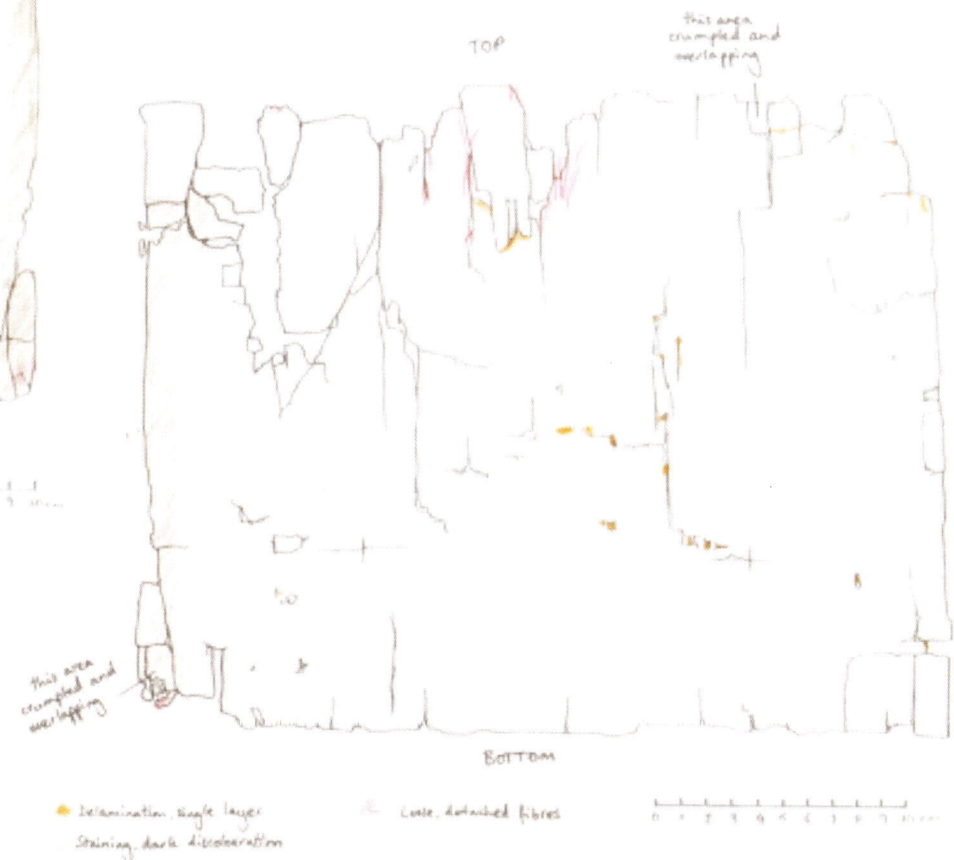

These drawings were annotated to show the location of different types of damage on the papyrus.

Conservation: condition of the papyrus before treatment

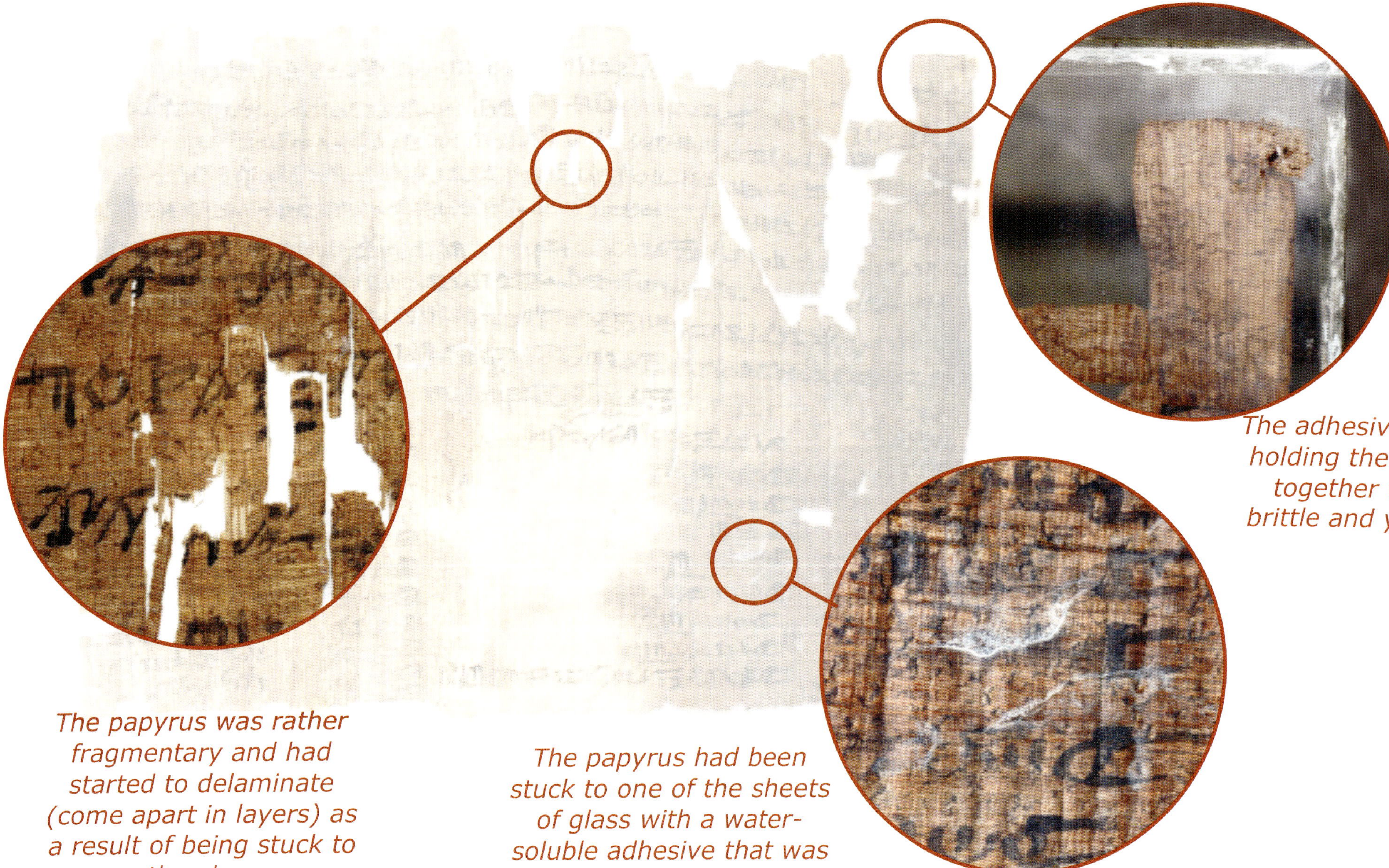

The adhesive tape holding the glass together was brittle and yellow

The papyrus was rather fragmentary and had started to delaminate (come apart in layers) as a result of being stuck to the glass

The papyrus had been stuck to one of the sheets of glass with a water-soluble adhesive that was now white and opaque

Conservation: unmounting the papyrus

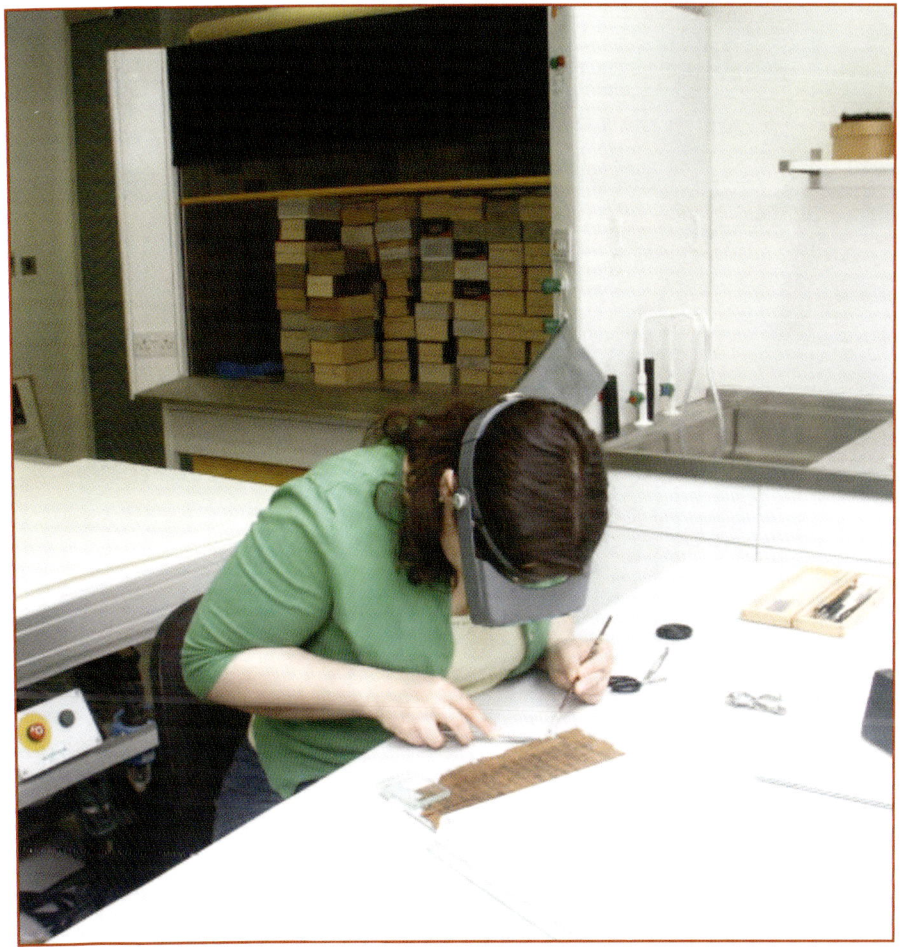

Water was fed underneath the edges of the papyrus with a paintbrush and it was gently lifted from the glass with a flexible spatula.

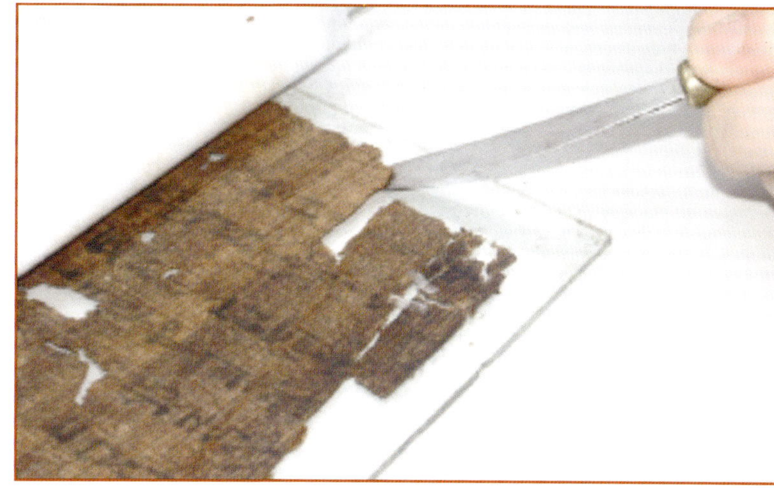

When an area of papyrus had been safely lifted from the glass...

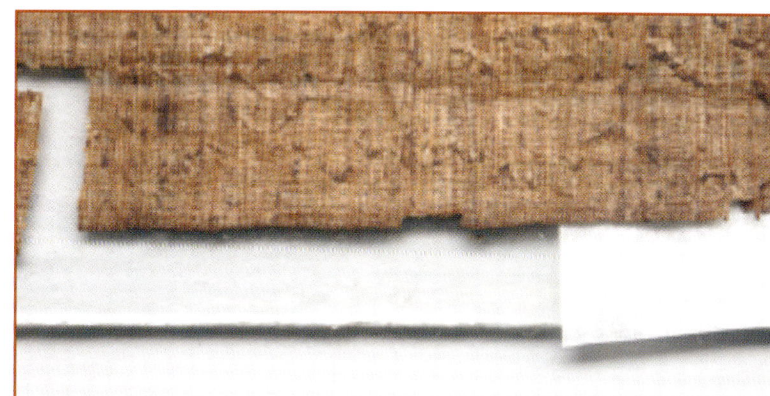

...a piece of silicone release paper was slipped underneath it to stop it sticking back to the glass.

Conservation: spot-testing the ink

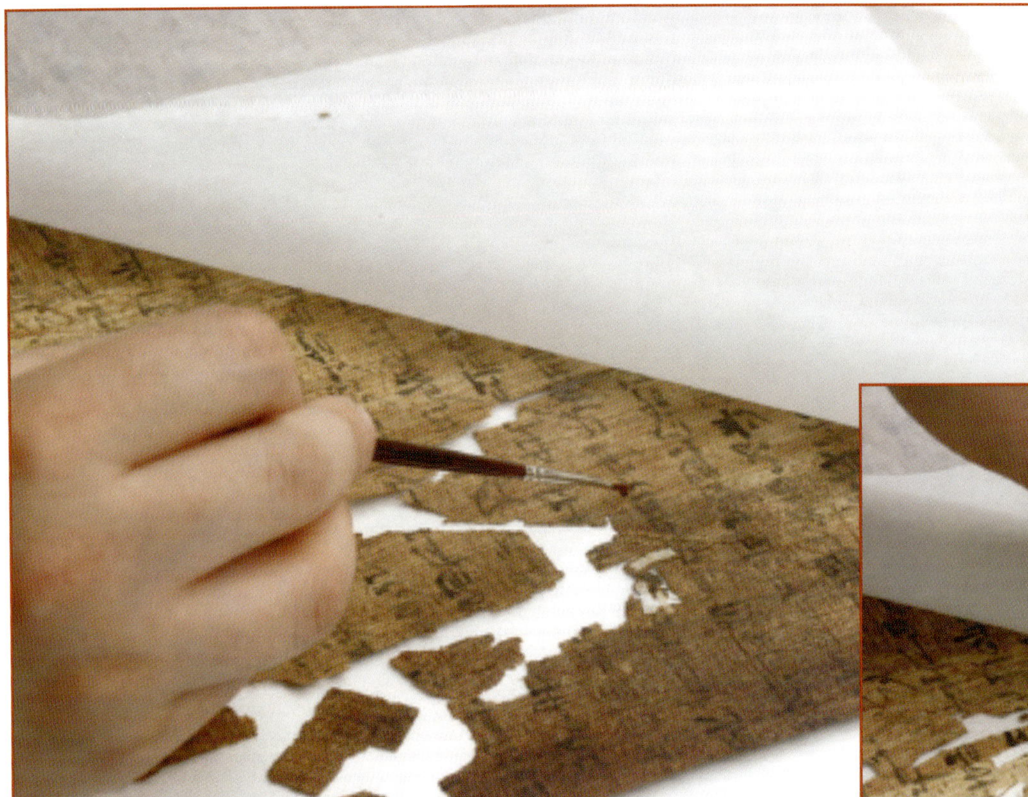

The black ink was tested for fastness before treatment: a spot of water was placed on a small area (*left*) and a strip of blotting paper was held against it for a few seconds (*below*).

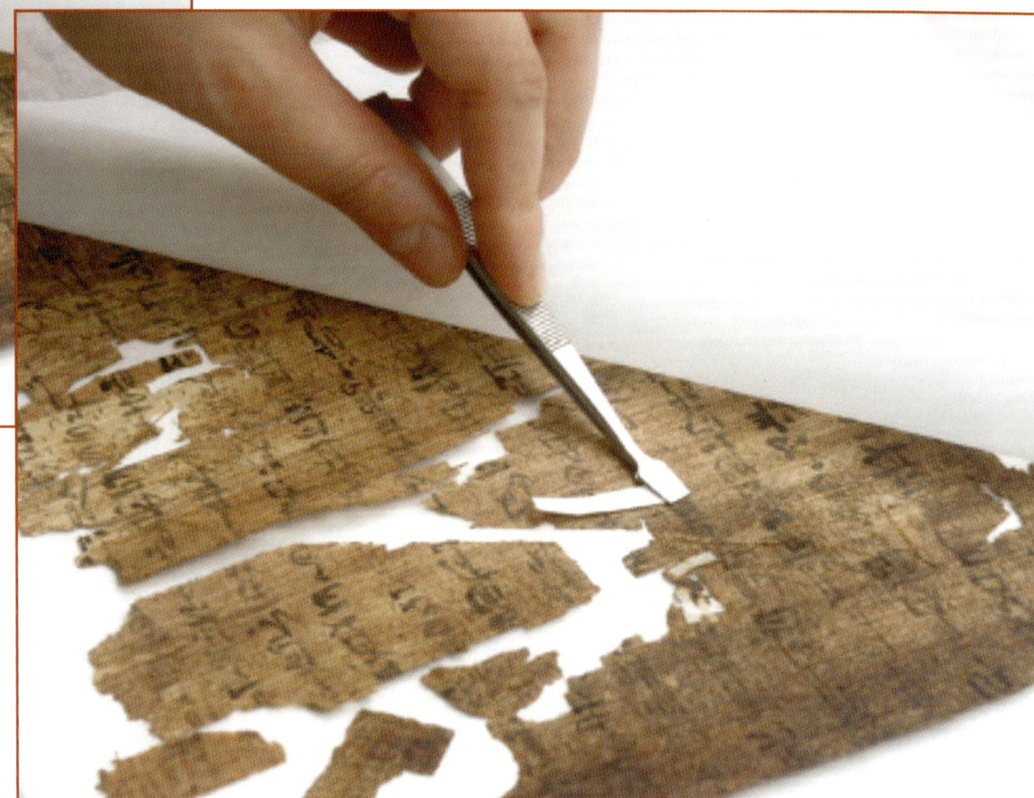

The black ink did not bleed on to the blotting paper. This meant that the papyrus could safely undergo treatments involving water, such as cleaning, humidification and reshaping.

Conservation: cleaning the fragments

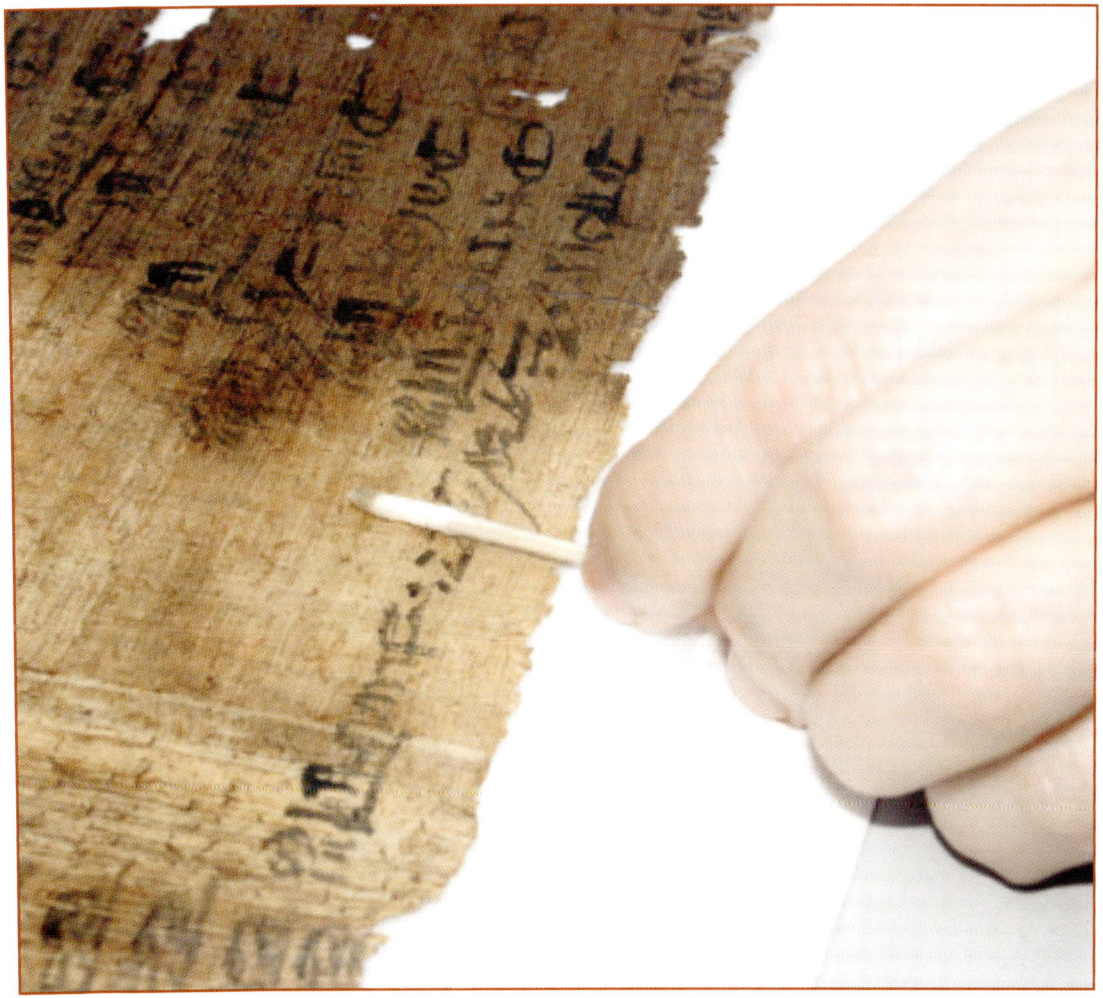

The papyrus was cleaned by hand. A cotton wool swab was dipped in deionised (purified) water and then gently rolled over the surface of the papyrus to remove any remaining adhesive.

The surface of the papyrus was very dirty. There were residues from the adhesive used to stick the sheet to its glass mount, as well as lots of dust from its years on display in the museum!

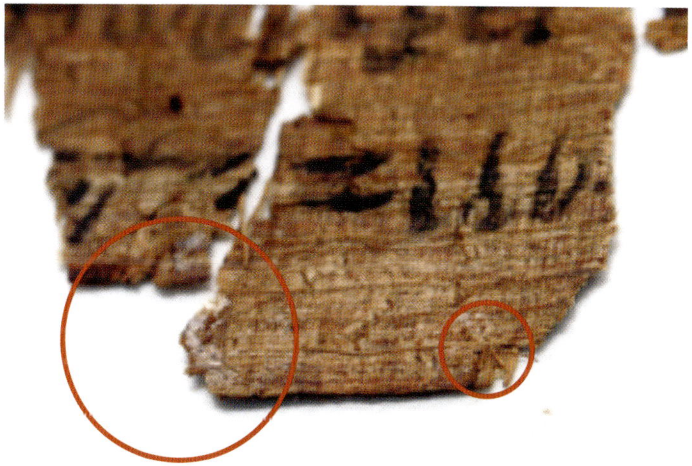

Traces of adhesive (circled in the picture above) are still visible on the papyrus fragments after they have been removed from the glass.

Conservation: humidification and reshaping

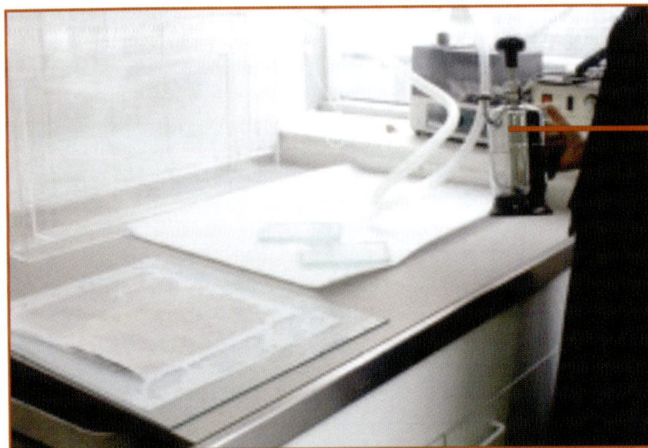

Water spray

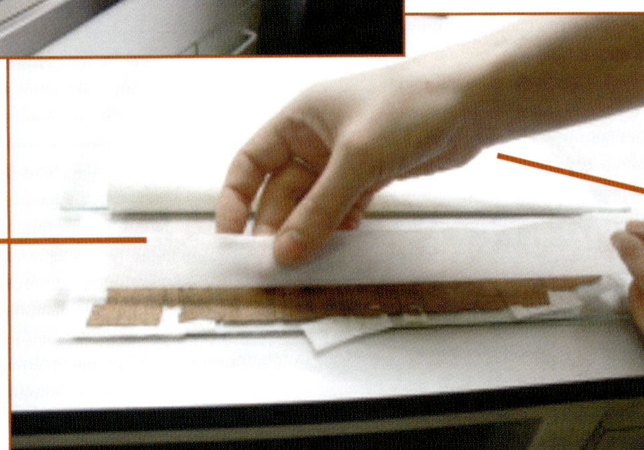

Bondina (permeable polyester sheet)

Blotting paper

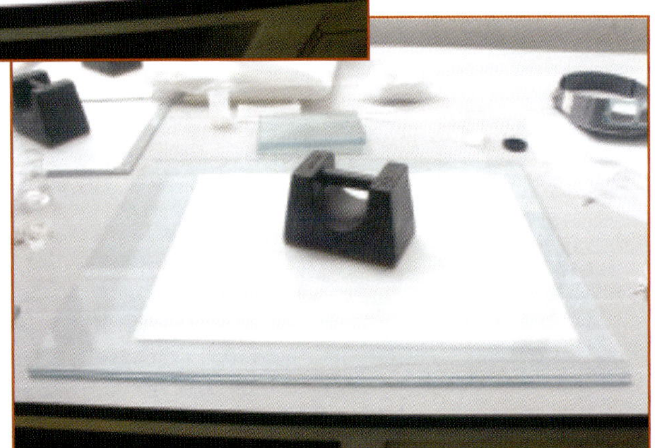

The papyrus was sprayed with deionised water to make it flexible, then pressed between two sheets of glass to help it lie flat.

Cross-section of the reshaping apparatus:

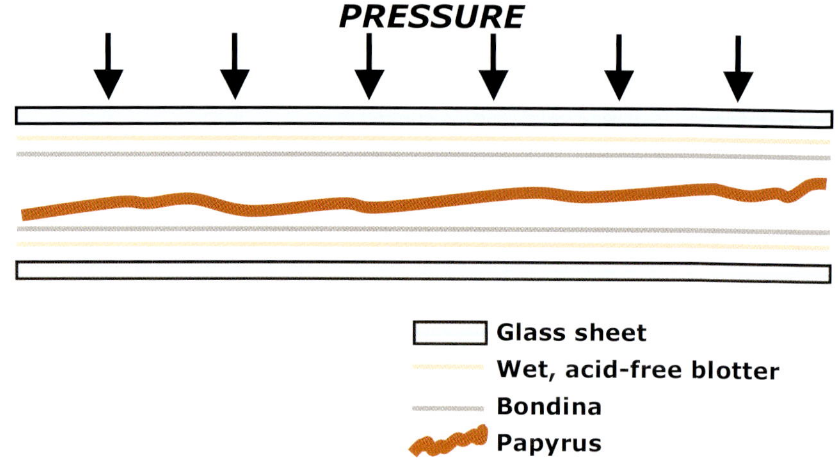

The wet papyrus was sandwiched between layers of blotting paper and bondina (*above*). The bondina acts as a separating layer and stops the papyrus from sticking to the blotter. The blotter gently takes up the moisture from the papyrus so it does not become too damp and go mouldy.

Conservation: joining the fragments

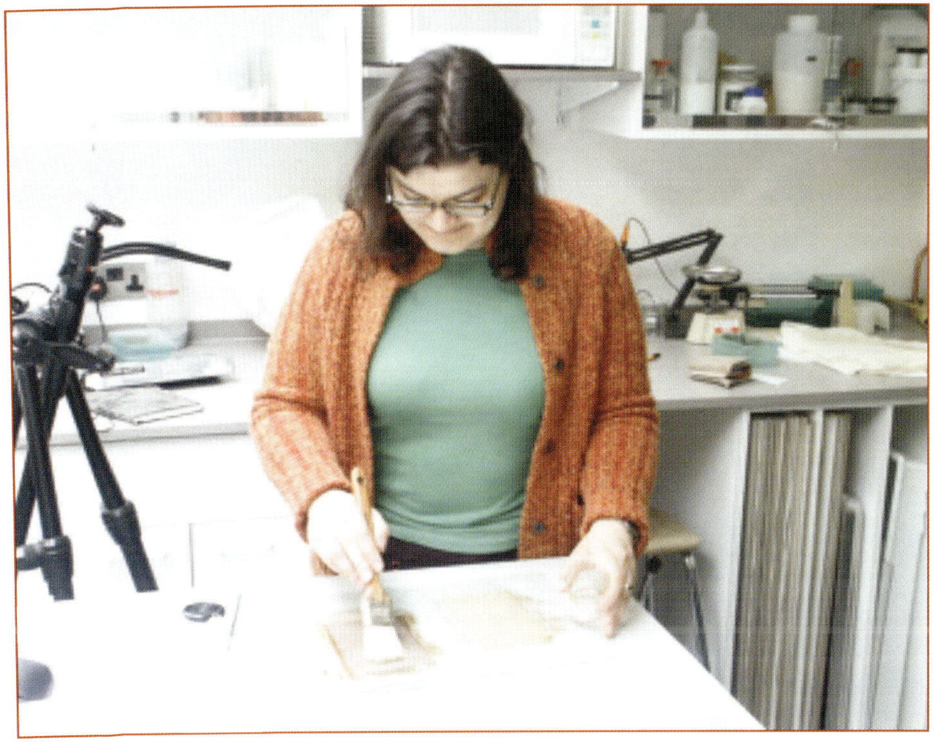

The papyrus was in several pieces, so it had to be reconstructed for display and support.

Fragments of papyrus are joined together with little tabs of Japanese tissue paper. The paper used for this is called *kozo* and is made from the paper mulberry bush. *Kozo* has very long, strong fibres, so it is ideal for this purpose.

The tissue is painted with watercolours so it blends in with the papyrus (*left*). The paper is painted through a layer of Bondina so the brush does not damage the paper fibres.

After it has been painted, the Japanese tissue paper is cut into tiny tabs (about 2mm x 7mm) to be used for joining fragments of papyrus together.

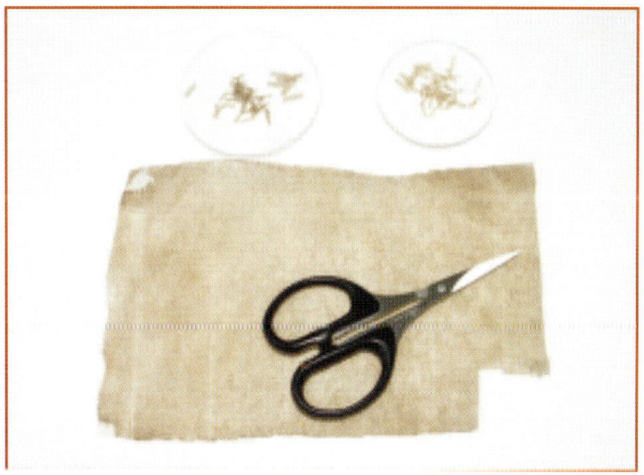

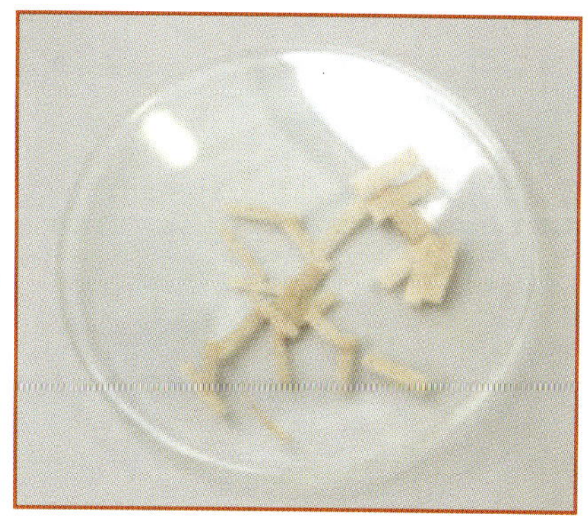

Conservation: joining the fragments

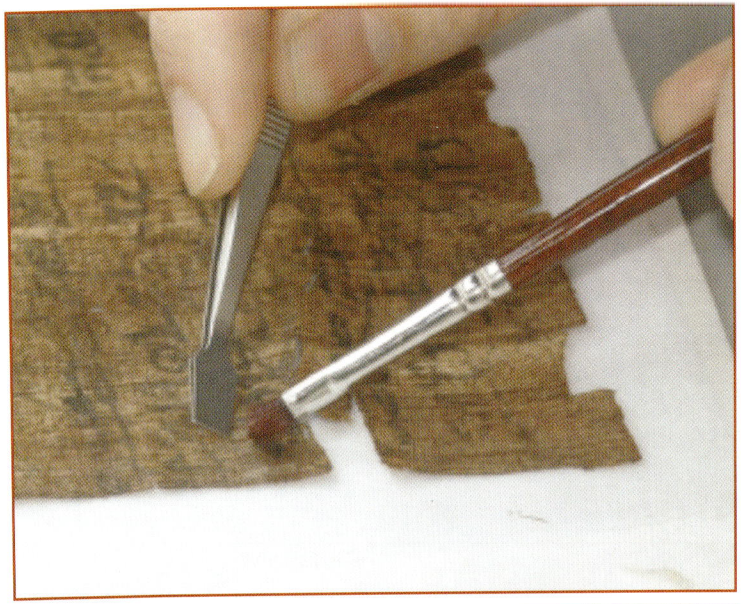

A tiny tab of Japanese tissue is coated with wheat starch paste, and then stuck down on either side of a break in the papyrus (*top left*). The tab holds the two pieces together like a bridge (*bottom left*).

It is important to place the tabs where they will not obscure text or images (*below*).

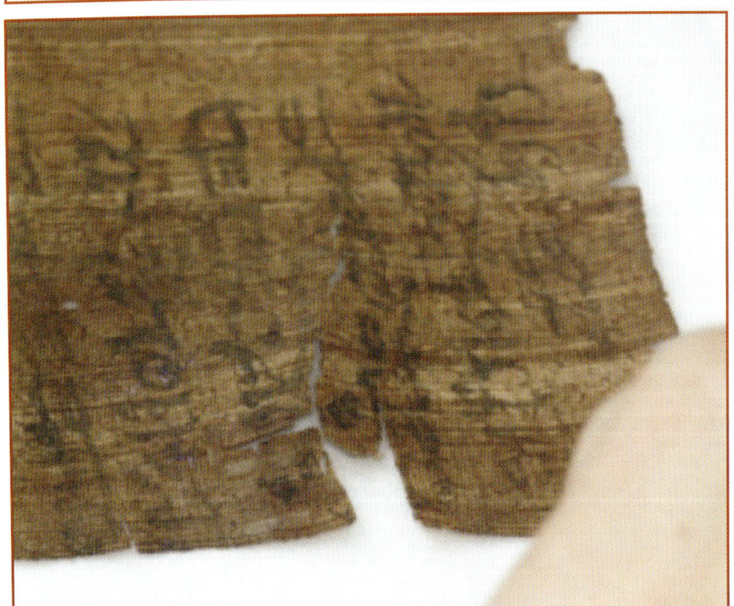

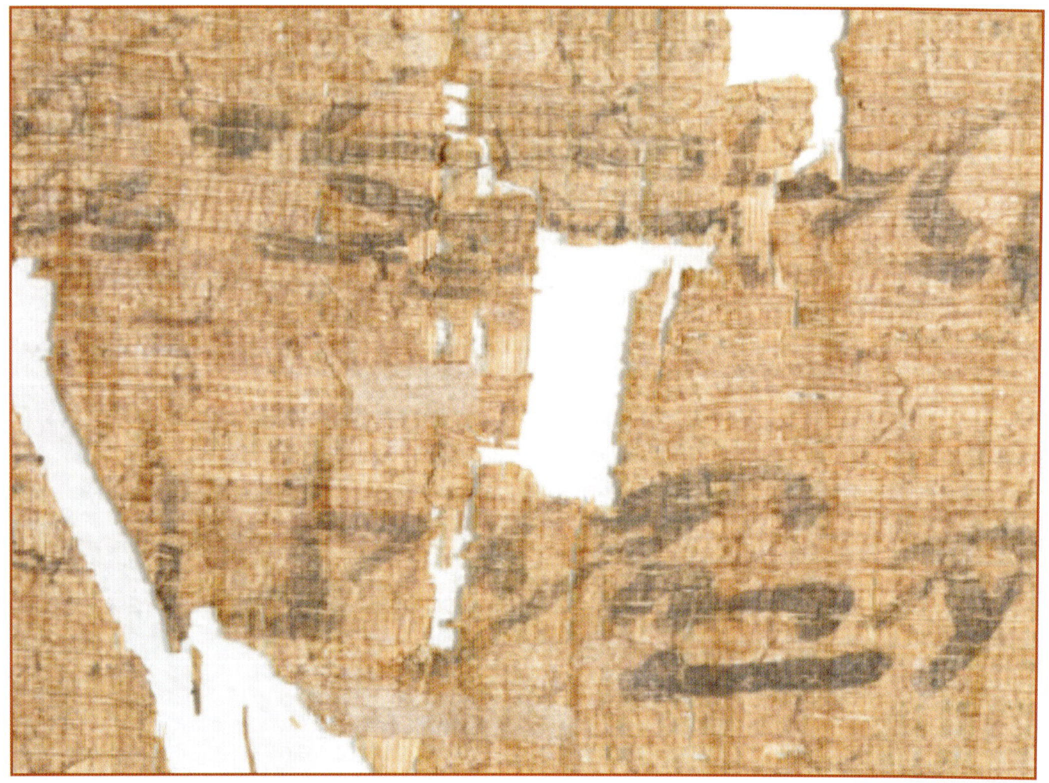

Conservation: checking the joins

The fibrous structure of papyrus means that it is very easy to check whether joins between pieces have been aligned correctly. The fibres on the fragments shown below match up on either side of the join, so it is a good join.

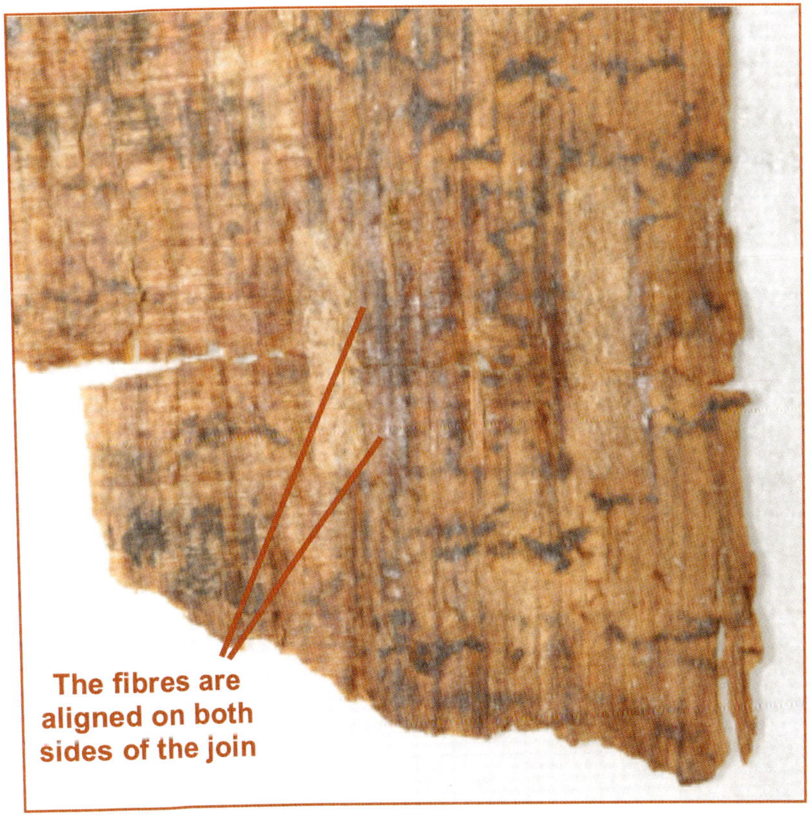

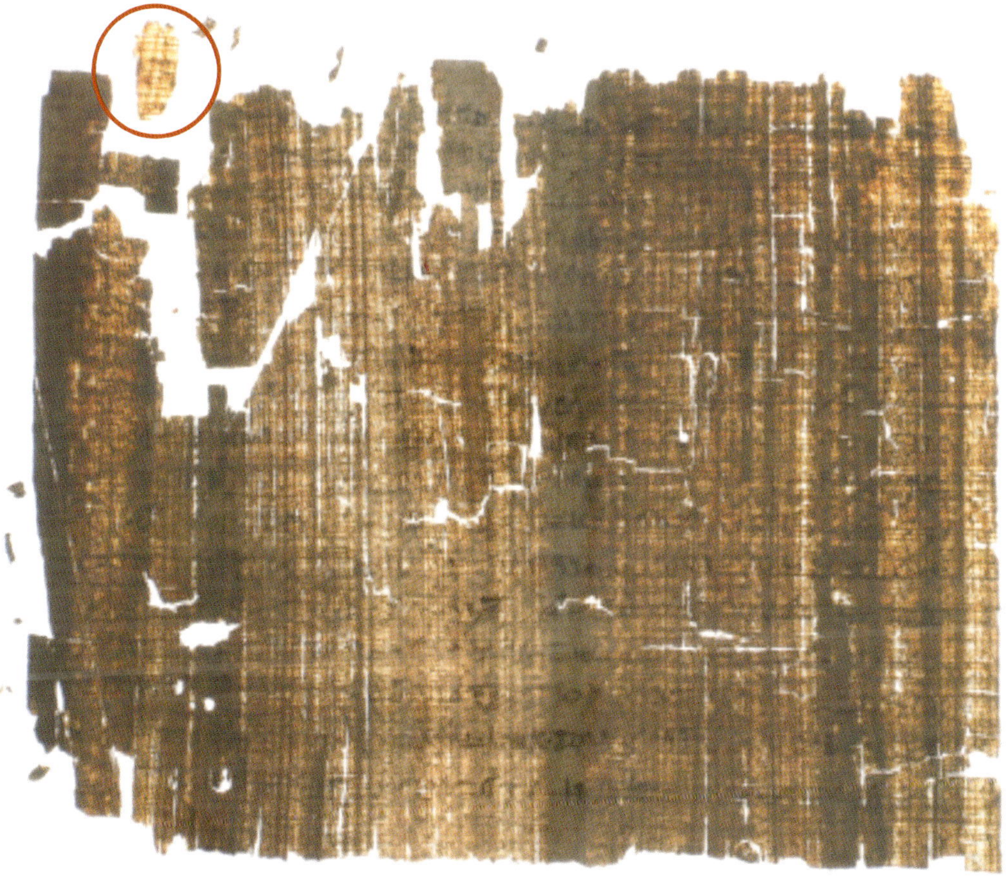

Because papyrus is so thin, useful information can be gathered by looking at it with transmitted light. The circled fragment above does not fit in anywhere with the rest of the papyrus, and it is a completely different thickness and colour — so it is probably from a different papyrus altogether!

Mounting: securing the papyrus

The papyrus was mounted between two thin (3mm) sheets of glass. The glass was cleaned carefully first, as any dust or smears are very difficult to remove once the papyrus has been positioned.

The papyrus is secured to the glass using more tabs of Japanese tissue paper. Loose fragments are mounted below the papyrus.

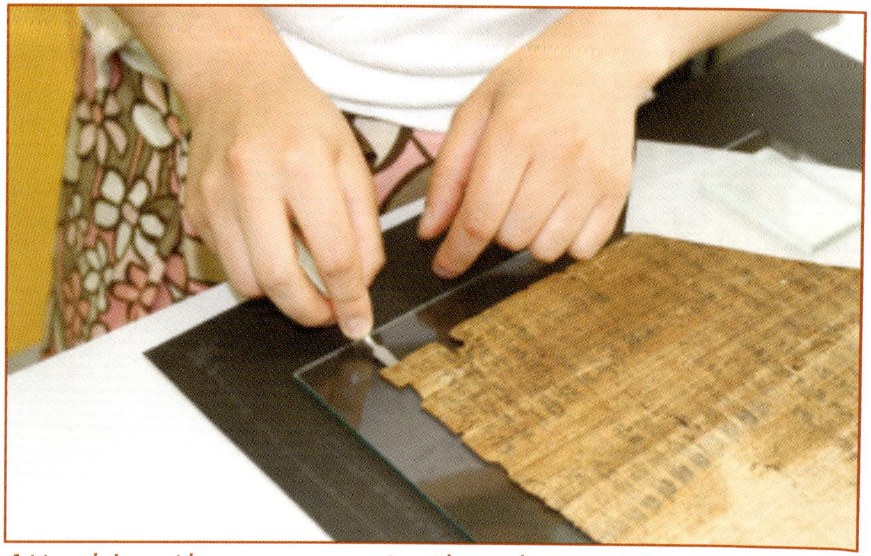

Attaching the papyrus to the glass with paper tabs.

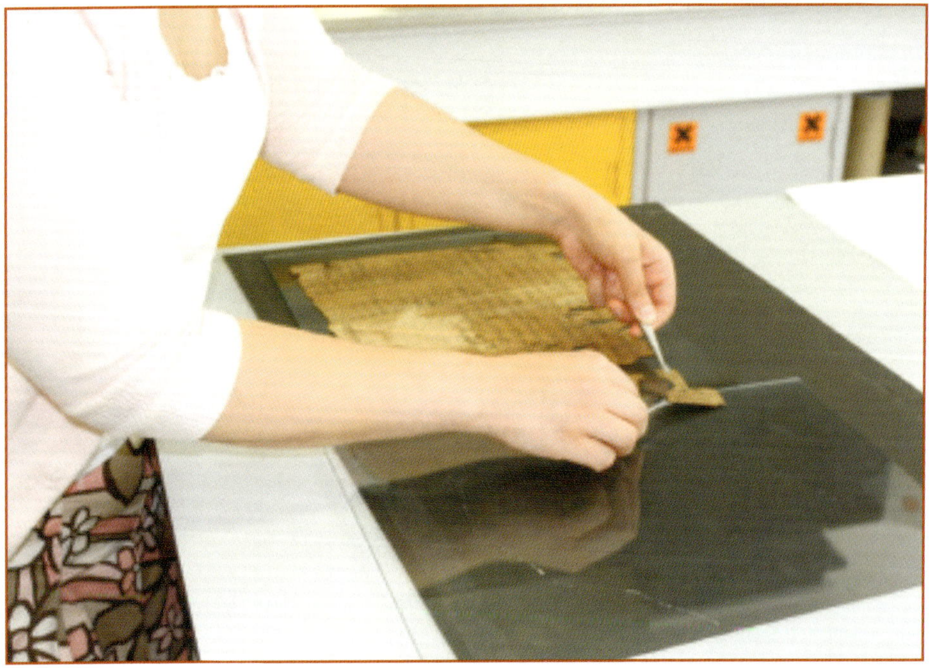

The papyrus is transferred to the cleaned glass.

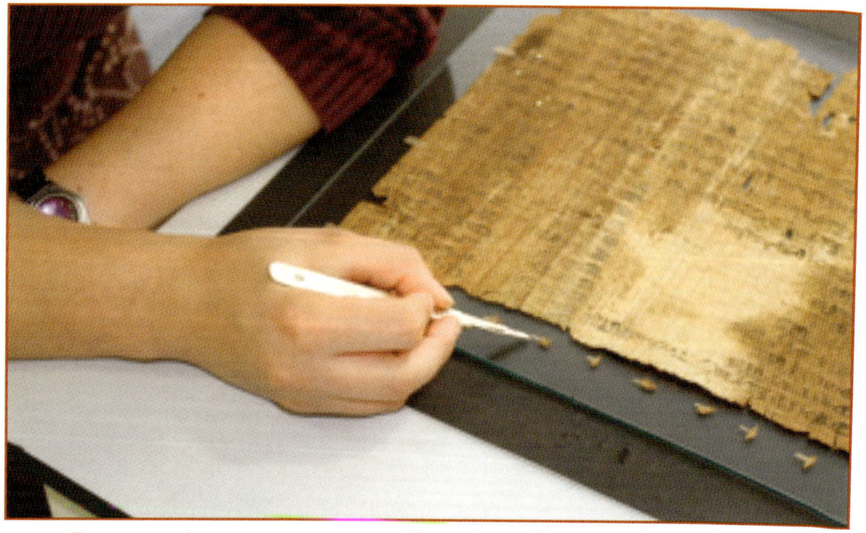

Removing excess adhesive from the glass.

Mounting: binding the edges of the glass

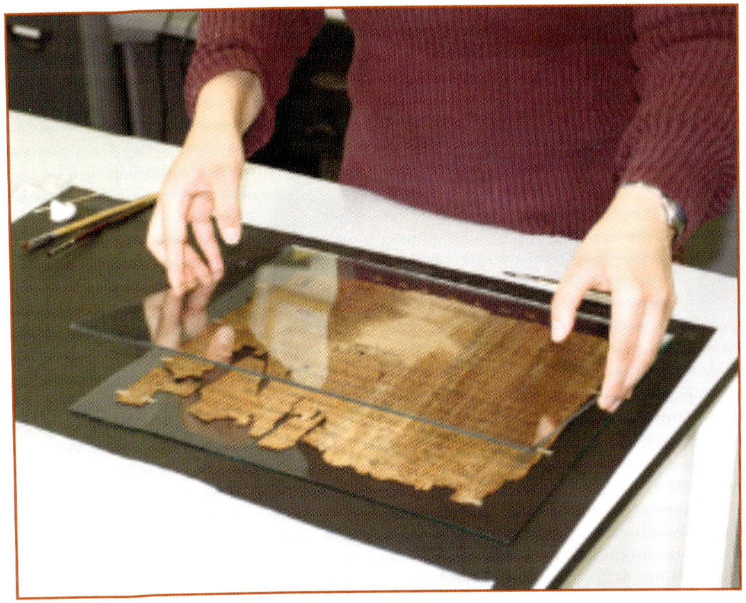

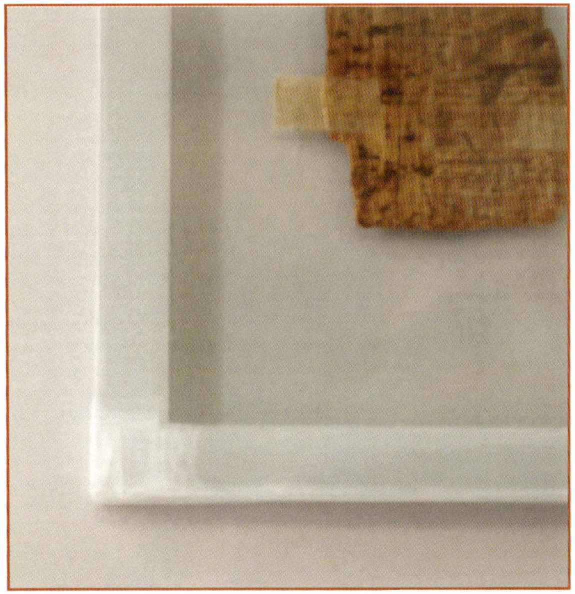

The second sheet of glass is carefully placed on top of the papyrus (*far left*).

The glass is sealed around the edges with a double layer of strong, clear, pressure-sensitive adhesive tape (*left*).

The tape is covered with self-adhesive fabric tape. This comes in several colours and gives the mount a neat, professional finish. Finally, the edges are trimmed cleanly, and the papyrus is ready to go on display!

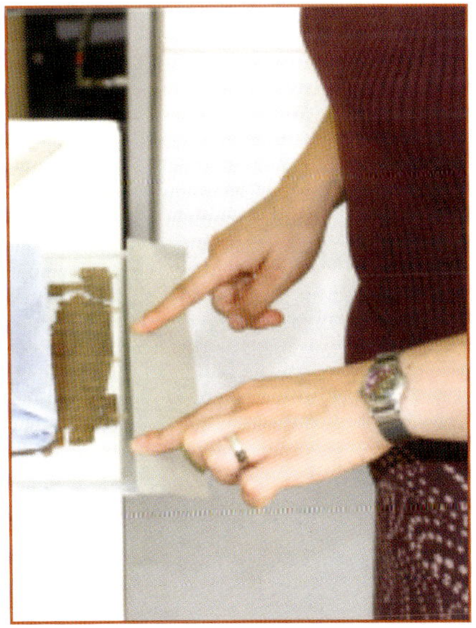

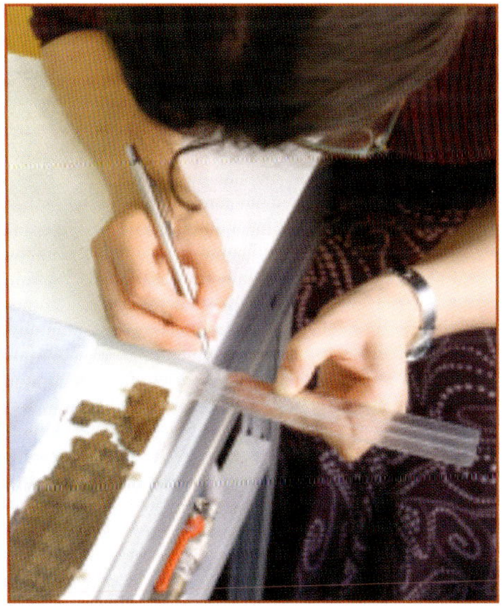

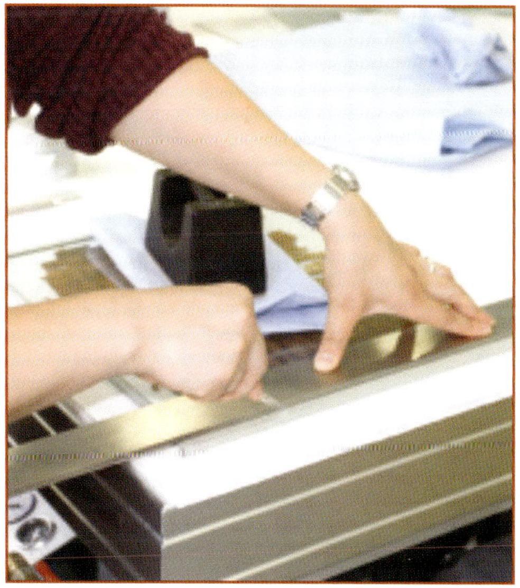

The papyrus after treatment

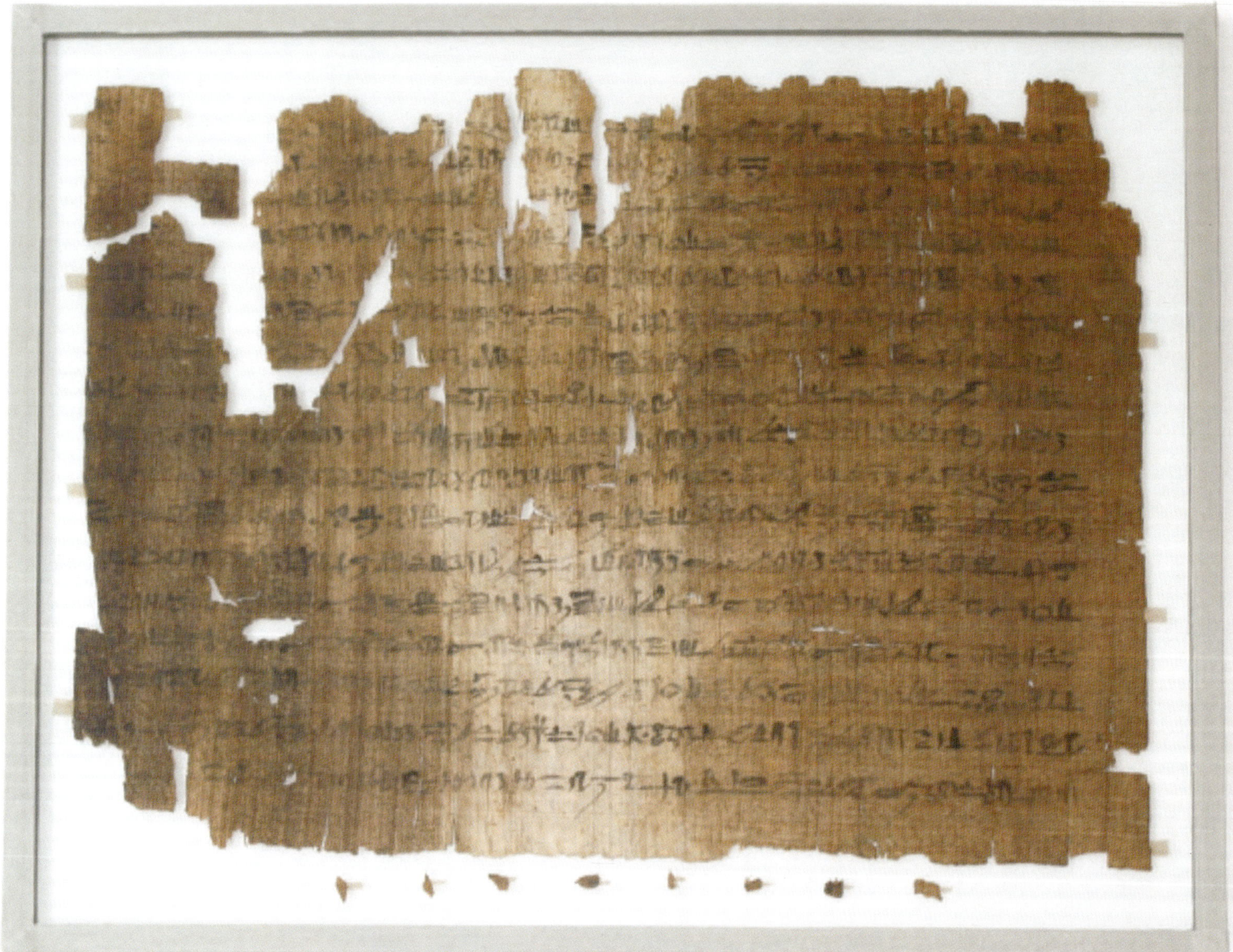